"I was deeply moved by the plain-spoken account of love... and loss. I was also much inspired by the way the author's love and faith guided him through the process of mourning – an experience that clearly brought a deeper appreciation for the gift of life and the blessings of loving human relationships. This little book serves as a welcome counterpoint to the way men tend to hide their emotions. Instead it celebrates joyfully the impact of a life and, despite the persistent pain of loss, to affirm God's grace at work."

~ Fr. Ron B. (Ret)

"Brian O'Connell did what no parent should ever do, bury their child. He shares his story with humor and love for his son."

~Michael Gershe, Founder
The Magic of Life Foundation

DADS
CRY
TOO

Living the New Norm

After a Father Buries His Child

BRIAN O'CONNELL

Year of the Book
135 Glen Avenue
Glen Rock, PA 17327

ISBN 13: 978-1-945670-92-3
ISBN 10: 1-945670-92-4

Front and back cover photos by Colleen O'Connell.

To purchase bulk copies, contact the publisher.

DEDICATION

This book is dedicated to everyone in my life who has ever made a decision that, in an instant, impacted my life as I know it. Specifically, my wife Raquel, my daughter Colleen, and my son PJ.

INTRODUCTION

For most of us there are few, truly "life-impacting" moments. Some are made in an instant... a flash, an impulse, where our lives can "turn on a dime." Others, are just presented to us by the universe, fate or God.

One of the biggest changes in my life occurred on May 6, 1984, when my son, PJ, was born in Los Angeles. Another occurred on May 6, 1986, when my daughter, Colleen, came into this world.

As a dad I did my best to provide for my family. In order to do that I had to relocate a lot to keep moving up the corporate ladder. When the war with Iraq broke out in 2003 (Operation Iraqi Freedom), PJ made the decision to join the Marines. Part of me was proud of him, but another part was scared shitless.

PJ served two tours in Iraq. Those were tough years emotionally. Raquel and I had tried to mentally prepare for the possibility of him dying in combat on a foreign battlefield, while at the same time attempting to push such thoughts to the back of our minds. We knew the reality of the situation. Life and death moments do not discriminate. They can happen to anyone anywhere, even close to home.

When PJ had completed his service as a Marine, we were once again the all-American family – mom, dad, two children and a dog... a typical middle-class family... until August 1, 2008.

Late at night on a winding road, near Hinckley, Ohio, PJ made a decision, in an instant, that would impact his friends for years to come, and change the lives of my wife, his sister, and me forever.

The following pages will tell my story, and how in one brief awful moment, that decision changed my life forever. This is the story of how my son helped me become a better man.

CHAPTER 1

FAMILY LIFE

We always referred to my son Purnell Jonathan O'Connell as PJ. He was born on May 6, 1984, in Los Angeles to the most beautiful woman I have ever met. Two years later on the same date his sister Mary Colleen came along. When they were little they thought they were twins because they shared a birthday.

I had arrived in Los Angeles about a decade earlier to pursue my dream of becoming a Hollywood stuntman. I had some degree of success, but not enough to feed a family of four. Rather than take a job waiting tables with other out-of-work actors I found gainful employment as a bill collector, repo man, plumber, painter, bartender, banker, and eventually as a certified equipment appraiser. Our little family moved around the country with stops in Atlanta, Milwaukee, and Cleveland, finally settling in Seville, Ohio.

When PJ was about three years old, we were living in a tiny two-bedroom house on 63rd Street in Wisconsin. This place was so small that if a spider farted in one of the bedrooms you could smell it in the kitchen.

Colleen and PJ had to share a bedroom. It was a tight fit with a crib and a bed in the cramped room, but we made it work.

One morning we heard Colleen cry but only for a second. About ten minutes later we heard her cry again. This time it was a little longer. It was one of those "I'm up so everyone else needs to get up, too" cries.

As we opened the bedroom door a cloud of white powder tidal waved out of the door. The entire room was filled with baby powder. We looked at Colleen and all we could see were her eyes and mouth. She resembled a Pillsbury Doughboy baby.

PJ had heard her first cry and decided to help out by changing her. Since he had watched us change her frequently, he knew the procedure. Remove the pajama's—check, remove the diaper—check, sprinkle some powder—check, check, check. If *some* powder was good, lots of powder must be better.

He was so proud of himself for helping us out and taking care of his little sister without being asked. It took us hours to clean up all the mess. Three decades later I'll bet there is still powder in the cracks and crevices of that old house.

PJ and his sister Colleen, 1987

Another time while still living in Wisconsin, PJ got mad at me. It was early one Saturday morning. He had no idea what time it was, and for him every day was the same so weekends held no special relevance.

My wife and I had been looking forward to sleeping in, but PJ came to our room and asked if he could have cereal and watch television. In a less than cheerful reply I told him, "No," and, "Go back to bed."

He stormed back to his bedroom and I heard him tell Colleen, "I'm going to go throw this at Daddy."

I had no idea what he was talking about but thought it wise to keep one eye open. I saw him peek around the corner and peer into our room. A moment later a projectile was launched at me. Instinctively I covered my face with the blanket.

(I'll give you a minute to picture this manly-man reaction.)

As I listened to PJ's feet scurry back to his room I looked around to see that he had thrown his pillow at me. Thank God for my catlike reflexes. To this day I'm grateful that Collen could not talk. I'm pretty sure she would have convinced him to throw a block or the baby lamp at me instead.

PJ and his sister Colleen, 1988

School was never PJ's strong suit. He loved the social aspect, but found homework and studying got in the way of having fun. Like most parents, I wanted my kids to have it better than me. I had graduated in the part of the class that made the top half possible.

PJ, the Cookie Monster

Purnell never got into trouble. He didn't get into fights, do drugs, cut school, or disrespect the teachers or staff. What he did do was the minimum necessary to get by. He once had a school assignment to identify five different leaves. The project had been assigned in September and wasn't due for six weeks. Of course he waited until the day before the assignment was due to *start* working on it. (I should point out that we were living in Wisconsin at this time, and it was near the end of October.... *and* we'd already had our first snowfall of the year.) He taped four leaves of varying shades of brown and crispiness with a small pine branch to a piece of poster board. He labeled each leaf including the pine branch, which he identified as a "Pine leaf."

One year while PJ was in high school he was required to attend summer school. He would ride the train downtown with me in the morning. His stop was the one before mine. He would have to exit and take a bus to the school offering his makeup class. At first I was nervous about him finding his way around on his own. My concerns were unwarranted. PJ really liked the adventure and independence.

After his class he would take a bus to my downtown office and we would have lunch together. It gave us time to catch up with each other. I don't know how much he learned in the summer class, but I learned what a great son I had. As we ate lunch, he would tell me about the guy sitting next to him on the bus that smelled like beer. I asked PJ why he didn't pick another seat and he told me he liked listening to the man tell stories about Viet Nam. He also told me about the lady with poor vision who had trouble finding the right bus. PJ would help her find her bus every day after his class, even if it meant he would have to take a later one to meet me.

My favorite memory of PJ is more of a gesture than a story. My wife and I were sitting in the living room watching television when PJ walked into the doorway, just about filling it up. He stretched out his arms like the Christ statue in Rio and said, "Love you guys." Then he turned and walked away.

My daughter Colleen was PJ's biggest supporter. Every time he needed to "lawyer up" she would always be there for him. I recall when PJ was grounded from going to a school dance. Colleen came to his defense, arguing that it would be the only time in his life that he would be able to attend this particular dance. She also pointed out how he was a big help around the house, and how I could count on him to walk the dog on cold winter nights when I was out of town. He ended up going to the dance.

Colleen went on to attend college at Ohio State and graduated (with a degree in social work, *not* law) in five years. I'm convinced it would have been four if she had not found a bar called "The Library." I vividly recall her telling me, "Oh Daddy, I'm so tired. I spent most of the week staying up late at The Library."

PJ and his sister Colleen, 2007

PJ graduated high school in 2002. His options for living at home were contingent upon either going to school full time, working full time, or a combination of the two. He attended a trade school for a very short time and then opted to become either a video game or paintball expert. Apparently his expertise was to be gained by playing them.

Eventually we got around to the: "My house – my rules" proclamation (I had turned into my dad). That announcement resulted in PJ joining the Marine Corps the very next day.

As a parent, my heart sank. It was a time when we were at war in Iraq. I now had a vested interest in a war that up until now had seemed distant in so many ways!

CHAPTER 2

LETTERS TO IRAQ

I promised PJ that I would write every day, and I fulfilled that promise.

PJ in Iraq

Each letter was filled with day-to-day events from back home. I was trying to convey some sort of normalcy while he was sitting in the desert fighting for his life in some town whose name I could not pronounce. I ended each letter with a joke or funny story. They were all signed, "Be a leader."

My foray into comedy started as a midlife crisis. I bought a motorcycle and took a comedy class because my wife would not allow me to date anyone else. The best advice I received from the class instructor was to work clean and try to write material every day.

My comedy career took off faster than many of my peers and before long I found success performing at corporate gigs and military shows all over the country.

By writing to PJ every day with a focus on trying to convey something funny I accomplished two objectives. First, it filled my commitment to my son about staying in touch, and second it helped me become a better comedian.

The following letter was sent to PJ in Iraq, composed on my birthday (so you, the reader, will know when to send me gifts). It should be noted that Sarah was our white German Shepherd, not a human.

July 18, 2005

LCPL Purnell O'Connell
2/2 Weapons Company
MAP BLUE
Unit 73085
FPO AE 09509-3085

Dear PJ,

Let me start out by saying, Happy Birthday to me. Your old man is 49. That means I've started my 50th year on this planet. By my calculation that leaves me with about 20 more to do something with my life. The downside is that I only have 1,040 weekends left. I better start making the best of them.

I'm so happy I got to talk with you yesterday. Colleen called and said you were turning off your phone after I didn't answer at home. Even though I didn't have much to say it was great just hearing your voice. Hang in there; you'll be home before you know it. By my calculation you will be there for 14 paydays. Doesn't seem so bad when you look at it that way.

Since it's Monday I'm going to take a few minutes and bring you up to speed on what happened over the weekend. Friday night your mother and I went to a movie and out to dinner. I had planned on taking her to Cleveland for dancing but we were too tired after dinner. Refresh my memory; was it you or me who wanted to leave the House of Blues concert early? Anyway, we saw "Wedding Crashers." It was pretty good. More of a guy movie because of all the stupid humor. I liked it more than your mother. We went to the 7:10 showing and got out about 9:30. We went to Medina and your mother didn't feel like going to Cleveland, so we headed across the street to Damon's. It was not very busy because we missed most of the dinner crowd. I had some bar-b-que chicken, rice, and a baked potato. Your mother had a salad and a baked potato. By the time we finished eating it had started raining pretty hard. We headed home, walked the dog, and called it a night.

On Saturday morning the repair guys returned our lawnmower. Something was messed up with the linkage. I had replaced the battery and the spark plug and it still would not stay started. They dropped it off about 8:30. Your mother started cutting the grass and I went to work repairing the water line to the toilet downstairs. We had a pretty good leak going and it was dripping into the basement. I knew something was up when I saw all the bugs in the basement pairing up. It was a mini version of Noah's Ark. I turned the water off to the house and went to the hardware store in Seville. When I got home your mother said the lawn mower had cut out on her. I started it up right away and we determined that she was just too short to use the mower. "Thank God you didn't marry a dwarf," I said.

I went in and finished fixing the water line to the toilet. Your mother and Colleen wanted to go shopping for my birthday present so I said I would cut some more grass. I had cut quite a bit when the mower cut out on me. That's the bad news because it means something else is wrong with it. The good news is that your mother is NOT too short to cut the grass.

I went in to call the repair guys but they closed at 2:00. It was 2:05 when I called. I left a message and decided to have a cold drink while waiting for them to call back. I wasn't sure if they would call since my call was 5 minutes after closing. I turned on the TV hoping to catch an episode of "COPS." I love the one where the guy steals the car and they chase him. Have you ever seen that one? To my surprise, the cable was out. Let's recap, my plumbing wasn't working when I got up, my lawnmower keeps breaking down, and now the cable is out. Oh yeah, did I mention that we still couldn't get online with your computer? At this point I think Osama has more creature comforts than me.

I decided to go out front and push the lawnmower to the barn. On a lark I tried to start it. The son-of-a-gun fired right up. I cut most of the yard with it until a storm blew in, forcing me to park it in the barn. I headed into the house and checked the cable. It was still out so I decided to go to DrugMart and refill my prescriptions. While there I would pick up a movie to watch on Saturday night. I took the Jeep and headed to Lodi. I had forgotten that this weekend was the world famous Lodi Corn Festival. That means it's free parking in the DrugMart lot. There are times I wish your Jeep was a monster truck. Anyway, I got what I needed and headed home.

Your mother and Colleen came home then and I was charged with grilling out. Burgers and chicken were on the menu. Everything went pretty well except for one hamburger that fell into the coals. I decided to fish it out and save it for Sarah. After about 10 minutes of using a long fork, tongs, a knife, and my fingers I finally got it. As I was putting it on the warming part of the grill the little bastard slipped through the warming grill and fell all the way down to the charcoal section.

I fished it out again and let it cool. Sarah enjoyed it. Later that night I started watching "Coach Carter." Halfway through the movie it started acting funny. Turns out Colleen owns that movie so I watched her version. See how I have progressed from watching movies we own when they come on TV to renting movies we already own? Next I'll be *buying* movies we already own.

After the movie ended, Colleen decided to go see Ben at Steak and Shake. She invited me to go along and asked to use the Camry. It is rare for me to go out at 11:00 but I said okay and I let her drive. We headed up to Brunswick and visited with Ben.

Sunday was pretty laid back. Went to church with your mom and Colleen. I picked up Ed and Jerry. I think Jerry forgot to take his meds because the priest had to ask him to stop talking.

After church we went to Bob Evans. When we got home your mother and Colleen went shopping again. Kathleen called and asked us to go to lunch because her and Michelle were driving through Ohio. Turns out they were already past our house. Sometime between Kathleen's call and you mother's calls to the house it started raining. That's when you decided to call. I was running from room to room closing windows so I missed your call.

Later in the day your mother and I went grocery shopping. She is going to make meatloaf for my birthday. When we got back we walked to the circle and then ate leftovers. In the evening I watched an Eagles concert.

That about sums up the weekend. I'll write to you tomorrow and tell you how my birthday went. You are going to have to write to us from time to time. The letters don't have to be long. A brief note just to let us know how you are doing. I'll try to send a care package once or twice a month.

Joke time:

An elderly couple goes to the doctor for a checkup. The doctor tells them that they're physically OK but they might want to start writing things down to help them remember. Later that night the old man gets up from his chair.

His wife asks, "Where are you going?"

"To the kitchen," he replies.

"Will you get me a bowl of ice cream?" his wife asks.

"Sure," he replies.

"Don't you think you should write it down so you can remember?"

"No, I can remember it."

"Well, I would like some strawberries on top too," she added. "You'd better write it down so you don't forget."

"I can remember that. A bowl of ice cream with strawberries."

"I also want whipped cream. You better write it down, I know you'll forget that."

"I don't need to write it down. Ice cream with strawberries and whipped cream. I can remember it."

Then he grumbles to himself and heads into the kitchen. After about 20 minutes the man returns from the kitchen and hands his wife a plate with bacon and eggs.

She stares at the plate for a moment and says, "Where's my toast?"

That's all for now. My prayers are with you.

Be a leader.

Love,
Dad

During PJ's first tour he had witnessed one of his best friends get killed by an IED. I dreaded every day thereafter. Beginning that very day, I followed all of the news I could on the TV, in the paper, and on the internet. I was in constant fear that a military vehicle would pull into the driveway and a couple of Marines would knock on my door with some horrific news.

Humvee gunner

I found myself praying for the parents of all the young men in harm's way, and a special prayer for those who would never hear their child's voice again. I hoped they were praying for me and my family.

PJ served his four-year stint with the Marines bravely and returned home safely.

Upon his homecoming PJ showed a renewed commitment to life and a sense of direction. He wanted to become a firefighter. I'm sure part of it was the adrenaline rush that comes with having a dangerous job, but another part of his decision was the sense of doing something good to help others.

PJ had purchased a motorcycle while he was stationed in North Carolina. He rode that "crotch rocket" everywhere. I knew he liked to push the limits with his bike. When we would ride together I would tell him to ride at his own pace and I would catch up with him down the road.

PJ on his motorcycle

He had logged enough miles on his bike to be considered proficient. In fact, he had ridden back and forth from North Carolina to Ohio on several occasions. He also made record time riding from Seville, Ohio, to Indianapolis to visit his girlfriend at school. He once told me he preferred his bike over women because his bike was pretty and fast, while some of his girlfriends were only one or the other.

As I said, I'm a former stuntman, but *that* motorcycle scared the crap out of me. I'll stick to my old-man motorcycle.

From my stuntman days

CHAPTER 3

IN AN INSTANT

It was the morning of July 31, 2008. I was finally getting around to re-installing the wood laminate floor in our foyer. Earlier that month my wife had left for Los Angeles to visit and help take care of her mother. I had promised to have the floor finished by the time she returned. Her plane was scheduled to arrive back home on Saturday, August 2nd.

There are two reasons why the floor project had taken an entire month. First, I'm much more proficient with plumbing tools than carpentry—and it is incredibly hard to install one of these floors with pipe wrenches. Secondly, I'm the world's biggest procrastinator. (Now we know why PJ waited so long to do his leaf project.)

My son had agreed to help with the project. In fact he had been on my case for weeks to get the floor installed. PJ is the type of kid (he was 24 at the time, and just completed firefighter school, but I still called him a kid), who likes to finish a project as quickly as possible. His expertise has always been demolition. If you needed something knocked down, ripped out or blown up, he was your man for the job. Today I really needed his muscle.

The floor had originally been installed by a professional, but the leveling compound had not dried completely and we had a potential mold problem. PJ and his best friend Jon had ripped up the old flooring and torn out the self-leveling compound weeks ago. I finally laid out the laminate pieces like a puzzle and now I needed PJ to help me slide them together to make the seams invisible.

We finished the job around 3:00. It looked good to us but it was obvious that a professional had not been consulted. Still, we were happy with our efforts. PJ headed upstairs to shower. He and Jon were taking their crotch-rockets out for a ride. They lived on those motorcycles. I always told them to slow down and be careful, but they were Marines with two tours of Iraq under their belts. The combination of youth and being battlefield veterans probably had them feeling indestructible.

PJ came down the steps, helmet in hand. I asked him if he would be home for dinner and whether he wanted me to wait for him. He replied that he didn't know what time he would be home, but that he would chow down on leftovers if he was late. He gave me a hug, kissed me on the top of my head and said, "Love you, Pops."

I said, "Love you too. Be careful."

"Always," he shouted back as he walked out the door.

The next morning, August 1st, the day before my wife was scheduled to return home from Los Angeles, at approximately 7:00 A.M., our white German Shepherd started barking. I assumed someone was probably walking down the sidewalk or PJ was coming back from Jon's house to help me clean before my wife got home.

Colleen had come home from college and was crashed on the couch because one of her friends had slept in her room. I know she heard the knock on the door but nothing was going to get her off that couch. Well, almost nothing.

I scrambled down the steps and opened the door. I was face to face with two policemen. One was in uniform, the other a detective.

"Are you Mr. O'Connell?"

"Yes," I answered.

"Is your son Purnell?"

At that moment my mind began to race. I had a pit in my stomach and a sudden emptiness in my heart. I was hoping and praying their next words would be, "Your son needs bail money," but I knew they didn't come to your house to tell you that.

I started thinking, *Please God, let him just be injured in a hospital.*

"May we come in?"

Those four words confirmed my worst fear.

The next few minutes are both a whirlwind of images and slow-motion replay in my mind. It was a collision of raw emotion and reality.

"Your son had a fatal accident at approximately 3:00 this morning. He and his friend Jon were both heading east on Route 303 and he lost control of his motorcycle."

I remember hearing a scream and seeing Colleen run upstairs crying.

"I know this is hard for you, but if it is any consolation, he died *instantly.*"

I managed to whisper, "Did he have his helmet on?"

"Yes," came the reply.

"Was he speeding?"

"Yes, we identified him through his wallet."

"How about Jon?"

"He suffered injuries when he hit some debris from the motorcycle. He's expected to have a full recovery."

I didn't want to believe it. I found myself hoping that maybe someone had stolen his wallet and his bike.

As I walked out with the officers, Jon and his parents pulled into the driveway. Jon was on crutches and his eyes were full of tears. We all hugged and cried. PJ was as close as a brother to Jon. They were best friends in high school and had joined the Marines on the buddy plan.

Jon had clearly suffered injuries when he hit debris from PJ's bike, but he still managed to flag down a motorist and ask them to call 911. Then he had done what I wish I could have done, an act that has left me both grateful and jealous—he laid down in the street and hugged PJ.

Colleen had been upstairs crying in her room. By the time she came back downstairs, the living room was full of company. Jon was still there with his parents. Emily—Purnell's fiancée—had arrived with a lady she carpooled to work with that morning. Colleen and I hugged and cried. In the back of my mind I kept thinking, *This is a horrible nightmare.*

Someone made coffee and I started to make phone calls. The first would prove to be hardest thing I ever had to do in my life. How do you call a child's mother and tell her one of her babies is *never* coming home?

I dialed the numbers slowly. I didn't have a plan as to how I would break the news. I would just let it come out.

Raquel answered the phone. It was approximately 5:00 A.M. in California. "Brian? What's wrong?"

Through the tears I blurted out, "PJ died last night!"

"Oh my God, NO, NO, NO! What happened?"

"He was in a motorcycle accident. He died instantly."

By now I could hear her family members in the background. She had been gone for a month to spend time with her mom who was getting on in years.

At that moment it was probably good for her to have all of her family around. But I don't know if she will ever forgive herself for being gone that month.

To this day I wish I had planned out my portion of that conversation prior to dialing the number. I wish I could have found a more sensitive way of breaking the news to the most caring person I know. I try to console myself with the fact that no matter how I had presented the horrific news... nothing was going to change the facts. A new norm had dawned on our family.

CHAPTER 4

THE FUNERAL

Things got chaotic over the next several hours. People were coming by, dropping off food, offering their prayers and sympathy. Family members started to drive in from the east coast, and fly in from the west. Plans were made to pick up my wife that night at the airport. Except for a few minutes at the funeral home, that ride home was the last time for the next two and a half weeks that my wife, daughter, and I would have alone.

We were kept busy picking up family members from the airport and train station. Funeral arrangements had to be made. The constant activity was a blessing. When you are so busy working out details, you don't have time to dwell on grieving.

I was amazed how many people came to the viewing and the funeral. PJ had just finished a program to become a firefighter and his entire class came by and presented us with his firefighter helmet. Marines arrived from across the country. *Semper Fi* personified. High school friends, teachers, and co-workers from a job he had through a temporary service all came to pay their respects.

You never really know how many people you impact on a daily basis. I don't know how he'd touched so many lives in 24 short years, yet somehow he did.

My son never really talked about what he'd witnessed in Iraq. Whatever it was, it changed him for life. I will always be grateful for his Marine brothers who came to the funeral and spent several days at our home. I finally got to learn about the man my son had become.

His brothers-in-arms told countless stories about PJ. (I had to adjust to them referring to him as "O'Connell"). Some were combat stories, but most were about his crazy antics both here and in Iraq. My favorite combat story dealt with PJ being out of uniform, wearing a Hawaiian shirt. A newbie arrived in Iraq and was getting his butt handed to him by a commanding officer. The newbie blurted out, "What about that guy? He's always walking around in that stupid Hawaiian shirt!"

The officer replied, "That's O'Connell... *he* makes me laugh!"

To this day I can't watch M*A*S*H without thinking of PJ.

The Marines also told me how much they enjoyed the letters that I had sent to PJ. They told me he would read them aloud, and they all looked forward to getting them. They said it made them feel like they were back home for a few minutes. Apparently, I was not just writing to my son, I was writing to an entire outfit.

They really enjoyed the jokes and funny stories that I included at the end of each letter. Here in the States, I was doing stand-up comedy, but getting laughs halfway around the world. You really never know how many lives you touch.

PJ loved to wear bright colors and was a huge hockey fan. In his honor, we all wore something bright, or Pittsburgh Penguins jerseys to his funeral. I know he was looking down and smiling.

Purnell was unconventional and certainly his own man. He was full of life and a carefree spirit. Stress was not an option for him. He was definitely never going to die of a heart attack. Comfortable wearing pink shirts, he even had a pink cowboy hat. According to my daughter he wore it because she hates pink. I tend to believe her because that is exactly the kind of thing he would do.

He showed he loved you by annoying you. Just the thought of him saying, "Dad, dad, dad, pops, daddy-yo, pops, dad, dad, dad…"

Until I screamed, *"WHAT?"*

As soon as I would yell, he would laugh and say, "Never mind," followed by another laugh.

I can't help but smile every time I think about it.

Chapter 5

When the Loss Hits

For me, the real sense of loss set in a couple of weeks after the rest of the world went back to its daily routine. With the flurry of activity complete, that is when people always start feeling the emptiness.

I know there are several stages of grief. There are a ton of books, written by professionals with lots of letters after their names, advising people as to how to cope with a loss and the grief. From my perspective grief is very personal.

I think many people assume that a dad is OK because they usually grieve in silence, especially around women, and certainly around other men. Friends often ask, "How is your wife doing?" Few, if any, of our friends asked her how I was doing. This left me feeling alone and abandoned.

I know some relationships end after going through a loss like this. I've heard the divorce rate after the loss of a child can be as high as 50%. I could not have gotten through it, though, without the support of my wife and daughter. Each of us grieved in our own way because we each had our own special relationship with PJ.

Colleen had lost her brother and best friend. Because we moved so much when they were kids, they came to depend on each other as the only consistent friend that would always be there. Now, PJ had left her.

My wife suffered a different loss. The relationship between a mother and son is special. Especially if he is the firstborn. I won't pretend to understand it, but I know it is real. I've witnessed it. My wife is very spiritual. She has embraced the position that PJ's spirit is always with us. She recognizes it in our grandchildren when they act a certain way or say something that has PJ written all over it. If a butterfly follows her around the yard on a summer day, she will insist that it is PJ coming to visit. I don't know if I believe it, but I find comfort in it.

For me, everything reminds me of PJ – the ding in the drywall from when we both moved the dresser, or the line from a movie he would always recite.

And that special song, there will always be those certain songs that move me to tears. I'm not ashamed to admit that from time to time, I have had to pull to the side of the road to regain my composure.

I wrote the following poem after a few too many beers, but it sums up my feelings when I allow myself to reflect. If I could read and write music maybe I would have a country hit on my hands.

Can't Drive with Tears in My Eyes

It happened again today
The feeling won't go away
Drove by the site of the crash
How long will the agony last
What price do I have to pay

Can't drive with tears in my eyes
So bad I pull off to the side
It just doesn't seem right
My heart is broken for life
And I drive with tears in my eyes

Don't know how I'll get through
Every song just reminds me of you
I've done everything I've wanted to do
Why couldn't it be me instead of you
How will I ever see it through

Can't drive with tears in my eyes
So bad I pull off to the side
It just doesn't seem right
My heart is broken for life
And I drive with tears in my eyes

The world around us keeps moving on
As if you were not even gone
I'm left to ask God why
With tears in my eyes
Why our plans had gone wrong

Can't drive with tears in my eyes
So bad I pull off to the side
It just doesn't seem right
My heart is broken for life
And I drive with tears in my eyes

The "What-if's" become part of your daily ritual. Holiday's, birthdays, weddings, graduations, and special events have a way of opening the wound to varying degrees. You silently wonder, *"Would this be different if PJ were here?" "What would PJ's wedding be like?" "I wish PJ could be here to see his nephews." "What would his children be like?"*

Sometimes the sadness is resurrected from unexpected sources. Whenever I hear or read about a child losing a life in a car accident, suicide, school shooting, or other tragic event my heart aches. Not only for myself but also for the parents dealing with a loss they never prepared for.

If your heart is not being torn open by the "What-if's," the days are filled with wrestling with the "Why's." Why did it have to be him? Why couldn't it be me? I've lived a full life. Why can't we trade places? Why didn't I get to say goodbye? Why couldn't I get one more kiss? Why not one last, "Love you, Pops"?

Some try to offer comfort by telling you to turn to God. They don't realize you can't turn to God because you are pissed off at him! I've had people tell me that God knows what you are going through because he offered up his own son for our sins. Well, that same God also raised his son from the dead because it was so painful!

You need family and friends who will listen to you as you ramble on and on about random thoughts and memories. Just listen. We really don't need you to say anything. In fact, there is *nothing* you can say that is going to make us feel better.

At PJ's funeral a lady tried to comfort me by saying, "I know what you are going through. I recently lost my cat." I know she meant well, but there is no way she could know what I was going through.

It takes a long time to come to terms with how your life is forever changed. The wound will never heal. All you can do is change the bandage. It really doesn't get any better. You learn to live with pain. You fake being OK. It takes a while before you can smile for real. You become a different version of yourself. There is a new sense of "normal" for you. The only people who truly understand are other parents who have lost a child. Yet, it's a club none of us want to belong to.

It doesn't matter how much or how little time you've had with the child... the loss is unimaginable. I spoke with a young mom who had a three-week old baby on life support. She had to make the ultimate decision. She prayed every day for some kind of guidance and finally decided to remove the tubes. Their last full day together was Mother's Day. The next day her baby girl would become an angel. In what can only be described as divine intervention the baby's last act was to open her eyes and smile. It was as if she were saying, "It's okay, Mom," and with that she passed on smiling.

Losing a child is unnatural. If a child loses parents, they are called "orphans." When someone loses a spouse they are called a "widow" or "widower." There simply is no word to describe losing a child. It's the only form of loss without a name.

CHAPTER 6

TRYING TO MAKE SENSE

Ever since my daughter was a little girl she would say, "It's not fair," when things didn't go her way. Like many parents I would reply, "Life's not fair." I can now say that with 100 percent conviction.

I can't speak for my daughter and her sense of loss. Only she can do that. But as of this writing she and her husband (a fellow Marine who served with PJ) have brought into this world two wonderful boys. She wants to have a third child. I suspect part of her thought process is that she doesn't want either of her boys to experience the feeling of being left behind that she goes through. In some ways it's survivor's guilt.

Years after PJ's passing I found out what his best friend Jon went through. The night of the accident Jon felt something pulling him back from being in front. Who knows if it was an angel, higher power, or God himself, but something was holding him back. PJ shot past him on the curve. The next thing Jon knew, he came around the corner and hit debris in the road. Jon thought he may have hit PJ.

He worried that he was responsible for PJ's death. He was overwhelmed with grief and pain.

Eventually Jon was overcome by a sense of light and warmth. It was as if PJ was standing over him and giving him a deep hug. Time had stopped. It was at that moment Jon's trust in God came back. It was PJ who made Jon believe in God again.

I don't think I'll ever have closure with this part of my life. There is a part of me that still gets excited with the anticipation of his bike pulling into the driveway, or having him walk into the house and give me a big bear hug. I allow myself to bathe in endorphins if only for the brief time that they wash over me.

The cold, harsh grip of reality snaps me back, and I'm left with memories and "What Ifs." At these times I force myself to concentrate on the memories.

As the years have passed, I've come to accept that PJ's spirit will be with me forever. When he was in high school he worked for a landscaper. One of his co-workers never brought a lunch. PJ found out that the guy had a family to feed and he skipped lunch to have more money for his wife and children. PJ started packing a second sandwich in his lunch so he could offer it to this man when they were on the same job together.

One day while walking to my downtown office I saw a homeless person sleeping in a storefront doorway. He was there every morning but was gone in the evening when I walked past to catch the train home. One morning I had a flashback memory to PJ packing a second sandwich and I started packing a lunch with $5.00 in the bag and leaving it in the doorway while the guy slept. I did this every weekday for months until I stopped seeing the guy in the doorway. I don't know if he moved on or passed away. I like to think that he gave PJ a high-five if he passed away.

I've since learned how PJ helped a young man decide to embrace a healthy life style. While working together at a temporary employment job after PJ was discharged from the Marines he met an overweight, out-of-shape young man who was being teased by co-workers. PJ befriended the young man and started eating lunch with him. Eventually, PJ talked the guy into eating a little less at lunch so they could have time to toss around the football in the parking lot. One thing led to another and the young man started eating healthier and working out at home after work.

PJ turned this young man's life around without ever mentioning diet or exercise. He simply became a friend and offered support. This same young man conveyed his story when he presented the football to me at the funeral.

I'll never know how many lives PJ touched. I'm sure there are stories about him that I'll never hear. Several years ago I received an ammo box filled with letters. My son-in-law reached out to some of PJ's Marine buddies and had them write to me. They told me about their interactions and experiences with him. These letters made me smile, laugh, and cry, but they also made me proud. My son had become a good man.

For many years I would watch *It's a Wonderful Life* at Christmas time—one of my favorite movies. Since PJ's passing, it has taken on more meaning, especially when they point out how you never know how many lives you touch in a lifetime.

Even if it's a short lifetime.

At the gravesite with my oldest grandson

CHAPTER 7

TEARS

I have asked all of my friends to celebrate "Hug your kids" days on May 6th and August 1st.

Not a day goes by without me thinking of PJ. I doubt I'll ever stop shedding tears when I'm alone with my thoughts. The difference is that sometimes they are tears of joy as I remember all of the good times.

PJ has served as an inspiration to me and has really helped me put life into perspective. Some of the things we worry about on a daily basis are not worth the bother. What is worth the effort is telling loved ones how you feel about them.

I will never again hear PJ say, "Love you, Pops," except in my memories, but I can connect with his spirit through simple kindness to others. It's easy to share the love within you. You don't have to be rich, famous, good looking, or popular to have a positive impact on others. Simply smile at someone, sit at a different table at lunch, or next to someone new on the bus, hold open a door for a stranger, let someone merge in traffic, or do something without first being asked.

PJ blowing a kiss

Maybe losing my son was God's way of telling me I have work to do. I don't know. I do plan on having a long talk with the man in charge when I get to the pearly gates. All my "Why's" have not been answered, and likely never will be until then.

Because of this experience I've had the opportunity to speak with church groups, youth organizations, schools, and others about how quickly your life can change. Some presentations have been focused on dealing with this type of loss. Others have been geared toward the results of an instantaneous decision. Many of the lectures remind the participants about how they can impact others through simple gestures of kindness and courtesies.

Many communities have support groups that can help with this type of loss. If not, maybe someone reading this book will be moved to start their own type of support group. If that happens, or if someone attending one of my presentations gains some insight that helps, I'll look at it as if PJ touched another life.

To my fellow dads I would like to say, I don't know why it hurts so much to lose a child. I do know this: the tears will continue for the rest of your life. Through the grace of God, over time, the tears will become tears of happiness brought on by joyful memories. Dads, it's okay to cry. You are not alone.

And remember, nobody is ever gone as long as there is someone to remember them.

About the Author

When he is not spending every spare moment with his grandchildren, Brian O'Connell can be found giving inspirational talks to youth groups, schools, colleges, hospitals, and churches about making choices that impact others.

He also speaks at grief support groups, especially those focusing on the loss of a child.

You won't see him as the leading man, but he does continue to work in movies and television as an actor and stunt professional.

Working under the stage name of Jay Boc, Brian continues to perform his clean stand-up comedy routine around the country for corporations and private events.

Connect with the author:

Brian O'Connell
c/o Dads Cry Too
8796 Westfield Road
Seville, OH 44273

www.dadscry.com
jayboc@jayboc.com

"On Sunday morning, the Mothers Club (formerly the Guild) of Beaumont High School held a Father-Daughter Communion Breakfast. It was a huge success providing our Dads and Daughters a morning of food for the soul, the body and the mind. Our speaker, Brian O'Connell, delivered an inspirational talk, Live to Love Every Day. It was a beautiful message to end a beautiful morning.

His message challenged the fathers and daughters to do three things: extend kindness, do something unexpected and tell loved ones every day that you love them. Everyone in the room was deeply moved and wanted to hear more! We left being thankful for the reminder to reach out every day to make a difference in the lives of others.

We highly recommend having Brian O'Connell as a featured speaker at your event. He delivers a moving and inspirational message that you do not want to miss!"

~Rosanne A., Beaumont Mothers Club

Made in the USA
San Bernardino, CA
02 November 2018